Children of the World

Poland

For a free color catalog describing Gareth Stevens' list of high-quality books, call 1-800-341-3569 (USA) or 1-800-461-9120 (Canada).

Author's note: For their help in the preparation of *Children of the World: Poland*, I would like to thank all the many wonderful people who helped with this project, including Heddy Moskaluk of Polonia Travel Agency, who suggested the Sczaniecki family and helped with lodging arrangements; the Sczanieckis themselves for opening their home and family to me; Waldek Dynerman for arranging for my interpreter, Agnieszka Zieborak, and her assistant, Sławik Kojło, who interpreted, guided, and drove me over much of Poland; and Janusz Tylman foremost for his hospitality while I was in Warsaw and also for his careful reading of the finished manuscript. I also would like to thank my husband, Daniel, and son, Noah, for their love and support during my travels and writing and photography endeavors.

Flag illustration on page 48, © Flag Research Center.

Library of Congress Cataloging-in-Publication Data

Holland, Gini.
    Poland / Gini Holland
        p. cm. -- (Children of the world)
    Includes index.
    Summary: The realities of contemporary Polish society are interwoven into this glimpse at the daily life of an eleven-year-old girl living with her family in the city of Poznan.
    ISBN: 0-8368-0233-0
    1. Poland--Juvenile literature. 2. Children--Poland--Juvenile literature. [1. Family life--Poland. 2. Poland--Social life and customs.] I. Title. II. Series: Children of the world (Milwaukee, Wis.)
DK4147.H65 1991
943.8—dc20   89-43181

Edited, designed, and produced by
Gareth Stevens Publishing
1555 North RiverCenter Drive, Suite 201
Milwaukee, Wisconsin 53212, USA

Text, photographs, and format copyright © 1992 by Gareth Stevens, Inc. First published in the United States and Canada in 1992 by Gareth Stevens, Inc.

Series editor: Valerie Weber
Research editor: Jamie Daniel
Designer: Beth Karpfinger
Map design: Sheri Gibbs

Printed in the United States of America

1 2 3 4 5 6 7 8 9 98 97 96 95 94 93 92

Children of the World

Poland

Text and Photography
by Gini Holland

Gareth Stevens Publishing
MILWAUKEE

. . . a note about *Children of the World:*

The children of the world live in fishing towns, Arctic regions, and urban centers, on islands and in mountain valleys, on sheep ranches and fruit farms. This series follows one child in each country through the pattern of his or her life. Candid photographs show the children with their families, at school, at play, and in their communities. The text describes the dreams of the children and, often through their own words, tells how they see themselves and their lives.

Each book also explores events that are unique to the country in which the child lives, including festivals, religious ceremonies, and national holidays. The *Children of the World* series does more than tell about foreign countries. It introduces the children of each country and shows readers what it is like to be a child in that country.

Children of the World includes the following published and to-be-published titles:

Afghanistan	El Salvador	Jordan	Saudi Arabia
Argentina	England	Kenya	Singapore
Australia	Finland	Malaysia	South Africa
Austria	France	Mexico	South Korea
Belize	Greece	Morocco	Spain
Bhutan	Guatemala	Nepal	Sweden
Bolivia	Honduras	New Zealand	Tanzania
Brazil	Hong Kong	Nicaragua	Thailand
Burma (Myanmar)	Hungary	Nigeria	Turkey
Canada	India	Norway	USSR
China	Indonesia	Panama	Vietnam
Costa Rica	Ireland	Peru	West Germany
Cuba	Israel	Philippines	Yugoslavia
Czechoslovakia	Italy	Poland	Zambia
Denmark	Jamaica	Portugal	
Egypt	Japan	Romania	

. . . and about *Poland:*

Surrounded by her extended family, Matylda Sczaniecka lives, works, and plays in Poznan, a commercial and industrial center. While working at school and studying three languages — Polish, Russian, and English — are important to her, Matylda much prefers playing and working with her friends and family. The traditions of her country surround her, from the flowers she brings as weekly gifts from her grandparents' garden to the memorials to the freedom fighters and war dead of World War II.

To enhance this book's value in libraries and classrooms, comprehensive reference sections include up-to-date information about Poland's geography, demographics, language, currency, education, culture, industry, and natural resources. *Poland* also features a bibliography, glossaries, activities and research projects, and discussions of such subjects as the country's history, language, political system, and ethnic and religious composition.

The living conditions and experiences of children in Poland vary according to economic, environmental, and ethnic circumstances. The reference sections help bring to life for young readers the diversity and richness of the culture and heritage of Poland. Of particular interest are discussions of Poland's tumultuous history, the exciting changes of the last decade, and the impact of religion on both personal lives and national politics.

CONTENTS

LIVING IN POLAND:
  Matylda, a Young Student of Languages 6

Matylda's Neighborhood and Home 10
Parents' Work at Home and Abroad 14
Matylda's Grandparents and Their Garden 16
School Days in Poland 20
World War II Still Affects Poles 24
Poznan's Old Market Square 30
Art and Culture: Pałac Kultury 34
Town Traditions 36
Sundays 38
Meals and Chores 40
Toys and TV — Relaxing at Home 44
Friends and Fun 46

FOR YOUR INFORMATION: Poland 48

Official Name 48
Capital 48
History 48
Government 54
Education 54
Population and Ethnic Groups 55
Land and Climate 55
Map of Poland 56
Natural Resources, Agriculture, and Industry 58
Currency 58
Language 59
Religion 59
Art and Culture 59
Sports and Recreation 60
Warsaw 60
Poles in North America 60
Glossary of Important Terms 61
Glossary of Useful Polish Terms 61
More Books about Poland 61
Things to Do — Research Projects and Activities 62
Index 63

LIVING IN POLAND:
Matylda, a Young Student of Languages

Matylda Sczaniecka is an 11-year-old girl from Poznan, the capital city of Poznan Province in Poland's central plains region. Her apartment is on the top floor of a four-story, walk-up apartment building. She lives with her mother, Alicja Sczaniecka, who is a child psychologist, her father, Bolek Sczaniecki, who is a physicist, and her pet schnauzer, Babsy, who is her best friend.

In Polish, family names typically end with "i" for males and with "a" for females. So Bolek's last name is Sczaniecki (schah-nee-ET-skee), while Matylda and her mother's name is Sczaniecka (schah-nee-ET-skuh).

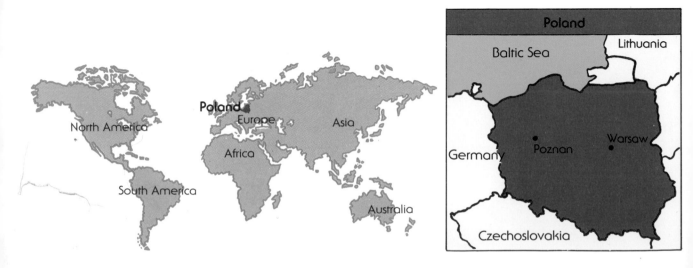

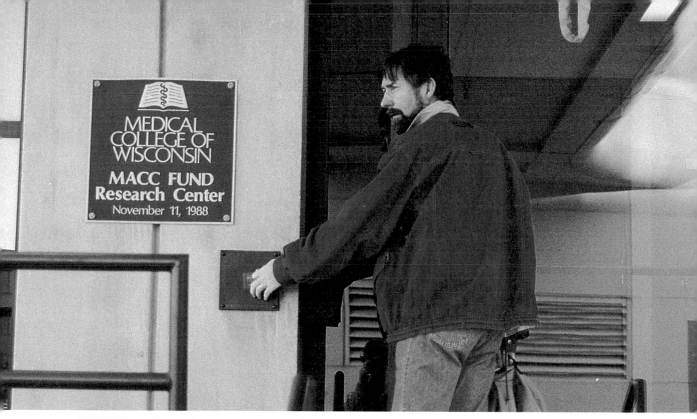

During one year abroad, Bolek did research in Milwaukee, Wisconsin.

Bolek's work sometimes takes him to other countries. Last year, Matylda and her mother joined him in the United States, where Matylda learned English. It was her second visit there.

Now she is glad to be back home in Poland, where she will study Russian as well as Polish in school. She knows her father will finish his project and be home in time for Christmas, her favorite holiday.

Matylda and her mother like to walk to church even on wet autumn days.

As in most Polish cities, church spires dominate Poznan's skyline.

Matylda tries to keep Babsy on a short leash as they pass their neighbors' gardens.

Matylda's Neighborhood and Home

Every morning, Babsy wakes Matylda, ready to go for a walk.
Matylda doesn't mind. She likes to run down the four flights of
stairs, matching her own scampering feet to her dog's quick steps.
Matylda takes Babsy past the playground behind the apartments,
around the sandbox and climbing equipment, and out onto the
grassy field. Soon, the bushes and trees hide them. Now they
are in their own quiet world.

Matylda prefers this acre of country land behind her apartment,
because on the other side of her building, the street is noisier and
less rural. A large electronics company stands across the road,
and at night, she can see its red neon sign from her bedroom
window. She can also see a huge soccer field from her father's
study. On Saturdays, crowds of people stream under their apartment windows, going to a soccer game.

Even in big cities, Polish apartment buildings often have wooded paths nearby.

Apartment complexes are everywhere in Poland, even in the countryside. In fact, more than half of all Polish families now live in apartments. These buildings are usually arranged in five or more identical blocks, which look out on communal playgrounds like those behind Matylda's apartment.

There are more apartments than houses in Poland mainly because so many houses were destroyed during World War II (1939-1945). When the Soviet Union took over Poland after the war, apartment buildings were built in both the countryside and the cities to give people a place to live. Each family had to apply to the communist government for housing. The space they received depended upon the number of people in the family. Even when they were able to pay rent, newly married couples often had to wait for many years to get their own apartment.

Most of the balconies in Matylda's apartment complex are divided in half, but some neighbors remove the dividing wall to share their space.

After waiting years for a bigger place, Matylda's family now lives in a newer and bigger apartment than is typical in Poland. Even their balcony is larger than most. Alicja has planted herbs in the window boxes and has plenty of room for deck chairs and space to hang out the wash.

Many apartment neighbors garden side by side in order to enjoy homegrown vegetables and flowers.

Parents' Work at Home and Abroad

As a child psychologist, Alicja works with children in a hospital. She tests them to check their intelligence and reasoning abilities. She also tries to find out how they feel about their family, friends, and the world around them. Alicja observes the children's behavior and, if necessary, does therapy with them to help them with their emotional problems. She also discusses the children's needs with the other hospital staff members.

Alicja works five days a week from 8:00 a.m. until 4:00 p.m. and sometimes must work on Saturdays as well. After work, she stops to do the daily marketing and then takes the bus home to make dinner and do household chores. It's a long day, but fortunately, Matylda is willing to help out at home.

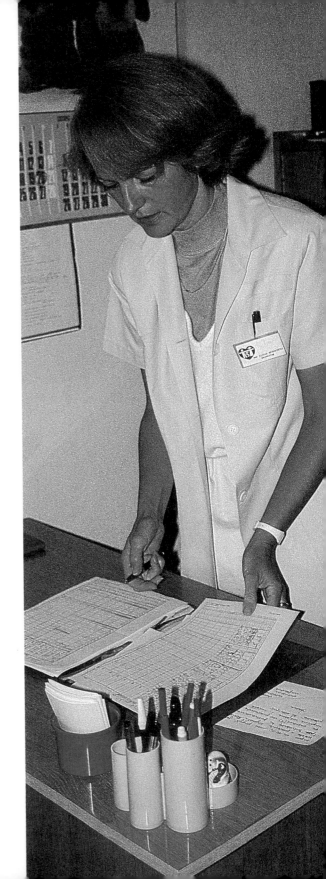

Alicja looks over the test results of one of her patients at the hospital.

14

Bolek uses many machines and instruments in his research. This machine makes a graph to record information from his experiments.

Matylda's father, Bolek, is a physicist, a scientist who studies physics. He studied many years to earn his doctoral degree. Now he is Dr. Sczaniecki. When he is not doing research abroad, he works at the Institute of Molecular Physics, a research facility in Poznan.

Bolek is just finishing a year-long project in the United States at the Medical College of Wisconsin. He uses complicated machines to test his theories in the field of physics and then writes reports on his findings.

Above: Matylda's grandfather and aunt are interested in her news whenever Matylda comes to visit.

Grandmother always welcomes Matylda with a warm smile. ▶

Matylda's Grandparents and Their Garden

On Sundays, Matylda and her mother often walk over to her grandparents' house for a visit. Matylda feels at home in their large living room and adjoining dining room with the big table, where all the family activities take place. Her grandparents always ask Matylda about school and the languages she is learning. Long ago, her grandmother studied English, and she still speaks it well. She likes to encourage Matylda's English studies.

Matylda's great-aunt, her aunt Maria, and another aunt and uncle also live with her grandparents. When the family applied to the communist government for housing, they included as many relatives as they could. This allowed Matylda's grandparents, aunts, and uncles all to qualify for a larger living space.

Matylda's great-aunt tends the flowers in the garden with care. Matylda and Alicja love to visit here, where the Sczanieckis also grow vegetables for the family table. High hedges surround the yard, so it's very private. Matylda can never leave without her great-aunt cutting some fresh flowers for her to take home.

Flowers are an important part of daily life in Poland. They are always for sale in the city squares, most apartment balconies have flower boxes, and all the homes have flower gardens. It is customary to bring flowers to a home when you are

Matylda's grandparents' private garden has so many flowers to choose from!

In town squares all over Poland, flower sellers do a thriving business. These flowers are for sale in the ancient capital city of Cracow.

invited for dinner, or any time you want to show appreciation or sympathy or add a festive touch to a celebration. Traditionally, flowers are carried with their blossoms pointing down until they are given to the person for whom they are intended. People all over Poland also regularly put fresh flowers on war memorials and religious shrines.

School Days in Poland

Each weekday morning, Matylda and her mother say good-bye to Babsy and go downstairs together before they part for the day. Alicja kisses Matylda good-bye, and Matylda waves as her mother heads toward the bus stop. Then Matylda walks about six blocks, past the apartments and homes of her neighborhood, and joins her friends in the school yard.

After a happy summer, Matylda is not so sure she wants to go back to school. Her mother shows that she understands how Matylda feels.

On the playground before school, Matylda and her friends have a chance to chat with their teacher from last year.

On the first day of school, her fourth-grade teacher from last year comes to the playground to say good-bye. She won't be their teacher this year, and the girls are disappointed. They had been told that she would teach them again. Interesting and kind, she made school enjoyable.

Matylda and her friends are worried about having a new teacher. But their former teacher says that when they get to know their new teacher, they will like her just as much as they liked their old one. Matylda and her friends aren't so sure, but they decide they should give it a chance. A few days later, after spending time with their new teacher, the girls are convinced that their old one was right — their new teacher is a lot of fun!

Matylda's school serves about 350 children, with approximately 30 students in each class. The girls usually sit on one side of the room, boys on the other. All must stand to address the teacher, but mostly they are there to listen carefully, not talk. There is much to be memorized, and discussion is limited.

In the classroom, Matylda's friend Sylvia manages to get a desk with Matylda, so they will be desk mates this year. They listen closely to their teacher's explanations about mathematics and geography and write down their assignments in plain, ruled notebooks.

Since it's the beginning of the year, the classroom is undecorated except for a plaque of the Crowned Eagle, a symbol of Poland, hanging at the front of the class. Soon, the walls will be covered with Matylda's and her classmates' artwork and posters and maps of the countries they will be studying.

Finally recess comes, and Matylda and Sylvia walk arm-in-arm down the halls. When they get to the stairs, they pick up speed, running with their friends. Soon the girls are jumping in unison as their friends turn a thick rope. After recess, the rest of the day is spent taking notes and listening to lectures on science and social studies and practicing Russian and Polish.

Right, top: Like children everywhere, Matylda and her friends quickly talk to one another before the teacher turns around to face the class.

Right, bottom: At recess, Matylda watches the rhythm of the rope and gets ready to run in for her jump.

World War II Still Affects Poles

The first day of school traditionally coincides with a very solemn Polish holiday. September 1st marks the day when Nazi Germany's leader, Adolf Hitler, invaded Poland and so began World War II. Each year, all Polish schoolchildren are reminded of how close they came to losing their country to the Nazis and how many Polish men and women died. Many take the time to put fresh flowers on the graves of those who died and on the statues and memorials to those who resisted the Nazis. This year, because September 1st falls on a weekend, Matylda's school will not have a formal service commemorating the start of World War II.

Poland was once a center of Jewish culture in Europe. At the time of World War II, 400,000 Jews lived in Warsaw alone. The Nazis systematically tried to destroy this culture, putting Jews and other Poles into concentration camps such as Auschwitz. Over three million Jews were killed in Poland alone.

AUSCHWITZ 1940-1945

-NAJWIĘKSZY HITLEROWSKI OBÓZ KONCENTRACYJNY
DLA WIĘŹNIÓW RÓŻNYCH NARODOWOŚCI
-OD 1942 R. BYŁ RÓWNIEŻ CENTRUM ZAGŁADY
EUROPEJSKICH ŻYDÓW

AUSCHWITZ 1940-1945-THE BIGGEST NAZI CONCENTRATION
CAMP FOR PRISONERS OF VARIOUS NATIONALITIES
-SINCE 1942 IT WAS ALSO A CENTRE FOR EXTERMINATION
OF EUROPEAN JEWS

Above and right: Scenes from Auschwitz, perhaps the
most notorious Nazi death camp. Triple-decker bunk
beds used to crowd three people to a bunk. A
museum now preserves this former concentration
camp so that no one will forget the horror of the
Holocaust, the Nazis' attempt to exterminate the Jews.

Left: In Warsaw, the Tomb of the Unknown Soldier, a
World War II monument, is lit by a perpetual flame
and guarded by soldiers night and day.

25

Even now, more than 50 years later, Matylda's family remembers World War II well. Matylda's father was a young child at the start of the war. He cannot forget how his family had to flee Poznan when the Nazis came from Germany.

Matylda's grandparents often tell her their family stories of personal courage and fear. The first country to be invaded by force by the Nazis, Poland is marked everywhere with memorials to World War II.

Because it was partitioned by Russia, Austria, and Prussia from 1795 until 1918, Poland had been an independent country for only 21 of the last 200 years — between World War I and World War II. After World War II, the Polish Communist Party took over the government, and Poland became a satellite country of the Soviet Union. The communist government assumed control of private industries and forced people to give up their individual family farms and join larger collective farms run by the government. The Polish people could only do what the communists decided, and no opposing political parties were allowed.

Graffiti like this tells what many Poles feel about Vladimir Lenin, regarded as the founder of Russian communism, and about communism in Poland.

26

This poster shows the Polish word for Solidarity. A shipbuilders' trade union, Solidarity helped lead the way to Polish democracy in the 1980s.

After getting free of the partitioning countries, the Poles grew increasingly tired of being run by yet another country. They formed new independent labor unions and, during much of the 1980s, worked to convince the Soviets that they should be allowed to vote for their own political parties. In 1989, Poland held its first free elections in almost 40 years, and few communists were reelected. The Sczanieckis proudly participated in the elections and are delighted to be rid of the communist government.

Because machinery is expensive, modern farming methods are rare in Poland. Many farmers still rely on horses to help till their land and harvest crops.

This horse-drawn cart circles Poznan's town square every Saturday, giving a quick tour of the restored houses and shops that frame the old cobbled streets.

Fresh flowers bring out the beauty in everyone.

Poznan's Old Market Square

On Saturdays, Matylda often visits her town square, where narrow row houses were lovingly rebuilt after World War II. She can go for a carriage ride, a tradition in the "old town" sections of most Polish cities. It's easy to forget that these historic homes were rebuilt from the ground up after World War II. They have been painted and finished exactly as they used to be.

Matylda has fun speeding around the square, past the town hall, listening to the fast clip-clop of the horse's shoes on ancient cobblestones. Matylda can imagine her grandmothers doing this as children, and her great- and great-great grandmothers before them.

Art galleries, ice cream shops, bookstores, and clothing establishments, all with a variety of goods, surround the town square. When the communists were in power, people could only buy things from state-run stores. Now, anyone may open a store, and many people are setting up small stands. Matylda likes to browse among the outdoor kiosks to see what they have for sale.

Wonderful breads and fresh fruits are usually available in Poland, but sweet corn is a special treat.

Matylda's grandfather used to run a camera shop just off of the Old Market Square. He began the shop when he brought his family back to Poznan after World War II. Since the government confiscated his farm after the war, he repaired secondhand cameras and typewriters and eventually developed film in a darkroom at the back of the shop. The government allowed some private businesses to provide services that were not available through communist collectives. So even under the communist economic system, Matylda's grandfather managed to run a private store.

Now Matylda's grandfather is retired. His daughter Maria continues the family business in a new location.

With the end of the communist government, the new government says it might return property to its owners from before the communists took over. The Sczanieckis wonder if they will get back the family farm and home.

Poland is struggling to change its economy now, from one in which the government runs industries to an economy with privately owned businesses. Although many proposals have been made, the current government is not sure how it's going to give control of businesses and farms back to the Polish people.

These are exciting times for the Sczanieckis and other families in Poland. Along with the changes in the country's government and economy comes an expansion of opportunities. Matylda may have more choices in her career and the way she leads her life than her parents did.

◀ Matylda joins the local shoppers in Poznan's restored Old Market Square, where mechanical goats come out of the clock tower every Saturday at noon to reenact an old town legend.

Matylda's first attempt at weaving.

Art and Culture: Pałac Kultury

Just off the Old Town Square is the Pałac Kultury,* where Matylda has studied dancing, art, and weaving. Her first project was to weave a picture of an apple, which turned out so well that Alicja displays it in their front hall.

Every major city in Poland has one of these "Palaces of Culture," an institution created by the Soviets during the communist rule. Now that the communists are out of power, Poznan's Pałac Kultury still houses a theater, a movie house, art galleries, and many classes for the public.

Although she no longer takes art classes at the Pałac Kultury, Matylda uses her skills to draw pictures for her father. She sends them to him in letters, and he hangs them up to remind himself of her while he is still far away from home.

Matylda's father admires the African mask that she made while attending school in the US.

* The ł in "Pałac" is a special letter that produces in Polish a "wuh" sound, much as the letter *w* does in English.

Even when she's not taking art lessons there, Matylda can go to the movies at the Pałac Kultury. ▶

Town Traditions

Every Polish city has its legends, with rituals to remind the Poles of their long and fascinating history. In Poznan, the story of the goats is reenacted at noon every day, recalling the time when a shepherd's goats strayed into the tower of the town hall. The shepherd climbed up to get them and saw from that height that a large fire had started in the town. He sounded the alarm and saved Poznan from burning to the ground. So every afternoon, two mechanical goats butt their horns together in the tower high above the square. The goats seem to leap into the air to fight, which delights both children and adults in the Old Market Square.

The city of Cracow's compelling tale about the Tartar's invasion of Poland is symbolized at St. Mary's Church. For the last 600 years, a man has come out of the high tower of the church every hour and blown a bugle call. He always stops suddenly because legend says the first trumpeter was shot in the throat with an arrow before he could finish warning the people of Cracow that the Tartars were invading. His half-played song is broadcast on the radio every day at noon all over Poland.

One of Matylda's favorite legends is about the terrible dragon Bazyliszek, which could kill anyone who looked into its frightening eyes. In some versions, the young prince saves the young princess from the dragon, and in other versions, the princess saves the prince. But either way, the clever royal child kills the dragon by holding a mirror up to its face. Bazyliszek takes one look into his own eyes in the mirror and falls over dead, demonstrating how evil can turn against itself.

Dragons appear in several Polish legends. Real flames roar out of this statue of a dragon near Wawel Castle in the ancient city of Cracow. ▶

Sundays

On Sundays, Matylda goes to church with her mother. Once a month, the sermon is especially for young people. All the children in the congregation must sit in the front of the church, while their parents and the rest of the parishioners sit behind them. Matylda and her friends try to sit quietly while the priest speaks.

He talks to them about the changes in their religious classes that will happen now that the communists are out of power. Religion can be taught in the schools again, so now they don't have to come to special classes at the church. Matylda's mother is pleased with this new arrangement because she won't have to worry about scheduling the classes after school.

Over 90% of Poland is Roman Catholic, and this religion is a central part of daily life for most Polish people. Even the smallest town has at least one church, and shrines to the Madonna, decorated with ribbons and flowers, are placed at many country crossroads. As the mother of God, Mary is particularly honored, and her image is found even more frequently than that of Jesus in Polish religious life.

Poles are also especially proud that the first non-Italian pope in almost 500 years, their former Polish cardinal Karol Wojtyla, was elected pope in 1978. Pope John Paul II — the name Wojtyla chose when elected — has strongly supported the Roman Catholic Church in Poland, even when both he and the Church were opposed by the communist government. Poles flock to see him during his frequent visits to his homeland.

◀ On his third visit to Poland as pope, John Paul II prays at the Fallen Shipyard Workers monument in Gdansk, which was erected to honor strikers killed protesting against the communist government.

Meals and Chores

Every morning, Matylda's mother makes tea and puts out the traditional Polish breakfast — several platters arranged with bread, butter, and tomatoes and slices of different kinds of cheese, sausage, and ham. Matylda can choose what she likes.

Although Matylda will bring a sandwich to school, no specific time or place is set aside for midday meals, and no Polish word exists for lunch. She and her friends will eat on the run at recess time, around noon. Breakfast and this snack will have to hold her until her mother gets home from work, between 4:00 and 5:00 p.m. Then she will have dinner, followed by a light supper around nine o'clock.

Matylda's mother, Alicja, likes to cook and is very creative with her ingredients. Alicja says, "You can't just take a recipe to the market and get what you need. In Poland, you must see what you can buy and then create your meal."

Matylda's mother has made a special treat for breakfast — deviled eggs!

Above: A gentle breeze from the patio cools the dining room as Matylda helps her mother prepare for company.

Right: Drying dishes is a good time to chat with Mama about the school day.

One of Matylda's daily responsibilities is to set the table for dinner. She likes to do this while her mother is just starting to cook. Then Matylda is free of chores until after dinner, when she clears the table and helps with washing the dishes.

Babsy always likes to lead Matylda and her cousins off their regular path.

It is also Matylda's job to take Babsy out as soon as she gets home from school and again after dinner. Matylda's cousins live in the neighborhood and often keep her company as she walks the dog. Matylda thinks this chore is more fun than work, and her cousins agree.

Matylda's home has a washing machine, so doing the laundry is easy. Matylda helps her mother hang the clothes out on the balcony, pinning them up on the line with brightly colored plastic clothespins. In damp weather, Matylda and her mother hang their wash on lines over the bathtub, where it can take several days to dry.

Toys and TV — Relaxing at Home

School is hard work. By the end of the day, Matylda is delighted to come home and spend some time playing with her cousins.

Matylda's cousin Krystina blows a bubble . . .

and . . .

They balance on Matylda's roller ball and play with her toys. Matylda has a large collection of dolls and ponies, lots of Legos, and a play land for little toy bears, so there's always plenty to do.

gets into trouble!

Sometimes Matylda and her cousins play Monopoly and pretend they are business tycoons. Matylda usually wants to be the banker because she likes to be in charge of all that money. Since capitalism is new to their country, it's fun to act out some of the ways to get rich — or to lose a fortune!

When cartoons come on, Matylda and her cousins relax in the living room and watch *Telewizia Poznan*, Poznan's television station. Some shows from the United States, such as "Wonder Years" and "Dallas," are shown with Polish dubbed over the English. There are cable stations in Poland, but Telewizia Poznan is the only official local station.

Even play can be serious when money is involved! Matylda thinks about her choices and makes her move.

Friends and Fun

Watching television is fun, but playing outside at school recess is better. Often, they play a version of Simon Says, with all the girls lined up on the steps.

The leader calls out the orders. Matylda and her friends try to do exactly what the leader says, but they must remember to listen for the words "Simon Says." Stepping up, jumping down, two steps, then one step — suddenly they are all trying to stop their jump in mid-air. Matylda is not the only one who gets fooled! Then she takes her turn as the leader. She knows it won't be long before she tricks someone else into making a false move.

Even though the teacher tells the children they are in school to learn academic subjects, Matylda thinks that these are the best minutes in the day, playing with friends. In spite of the hard work ahead, Matylda is glad to be back in school, because school means seeing friends every day and laughing and learning together.

Matylda and her friends get tricked by their leader at recess.

46

FOR YOUR INFORMATION: Poland

OFFICIAL NAME: POLSKA
(POHL-skuh)
Poland

Capital: Warsaw

History

Location has determined much of Poland's history. In the heart of Europe, it was often a buffer zone between the surrounding countries, which frequently fought Poland and each other on Polish soil. As a result, its borders have shifted continuously throughout its history. At one point in the 16th century, Poland was the largest country in Europe. At other times, it has disappeared from the map. Poland has had to be united within itself or perish.

In Cracow, boats dock on the Wisła River beneath the ancient Cracow Cathedral of St. Waclaw and St. Stanislaw, where, from the 11th century on, Polish kings and queens were crowned.

Poland — Where the Slavonic People Began

Even before the year 2000 BC, ancestors of the modern Poles lived and worked in the area that is now Poland. They were members of the Slavonic tribes. The Slavonic people who did not migrate to areas such as the former Union of Soviet Socialist Republics (USSR), Czechoslovakia, and neighboring parts of Europe stayed in the region and became ancestors of the people of Poland.

These Slavonic tribes were highly developed by the beginning of the Iron Age during the 7th and 6th centuries BC. They built fortified towns, grew grains, bred farm animals, and by 500 BC, were using wooden plows pulled by oxen. Over the next 1,400 years, the structure of these tribes changed from primitive communes to more organized communities and finally to separate states.

The Piast Period, AD 960-1386

The first family strong enough to rule a majority of Poles were the Piasts. They wanted to unify the states to protect their territories from other countries. They increasingly gained power until finally a Piast named Mieszko I (Mee-ESH-ko) was crowned the first true prince of Poland. Under his rule from AD 963 to 992, other nations recognized Poland as an independent country. The country took its name from the Slavonic word *polanie* meaning "dwellers of the field," because the majority of the Poles were farmers at this time. In 966, Mieszko I accepted Christianity, and Poland has been Roman Catholic ever since.

Mieszko I died in 992, and his son, Bolesław (BOH-le-swahv) the Brave, became prince of Poland. He united the tribes and brought more areas within Poland's boundaries. In 1025, the last year of his reign, Bolesław declared himself king.

When Bolesław died, his sons started to divide Poland up among themselves. Soon Poland was carved into so many small kingdoms that it couldn't defend itself against its neighbors very effectively. Germans, Czechs, Russians, and Tartars from Mongolia invaded Poland over and over. Although the Poles were divided during this time by their separate rulers, they remained linked by their common language and Catholic religion.

During the mid-1300s, Ladislas the Short and his son, Casimir the Great, organized Poland into a united kingdom once again. Economic conditions improved for peasants and nobles alike. The Wieliczka salt mines near

Cracow were expanded to become among the largest in Europe, providing one-third of Poland's state revenue.

Casimir strengthened the economy and government, but having no children, he was the last Piast ruler. He arranged for his nephew, King Louis of Hungary, to be crowned after he died. But King Louis preferred Hungary and did not concentrate on the job of governing Poland.

The Jagiellons 1386-1572

Throughout the Middle Ages, powerful Polish nobles often decided government policy. In 1384, they agreed to accept one of Louis' daughters as his successor if she promised to move to Poland. Although a female ruler was very unusual, Jadwiga, not yet ten years old, was crowned "king" of Poland. When Jadwiga was 12, the nobles made her marry Jagiello, grand duke of Lithuania. This allowed them to end their war with Lithuania and to concentrate on defeating the German Teutonic knights who continued to invade both countries. The nobles also made Jagiello accept Christianity, so the Lithuanian people would be Roman Catholic, too. In 1410, Jagiello beat the Teutonic knights at the great Battle of Grunwald.

For the next 200 years, Jagiellonian kings ruled a united and powerful Poland. They took over the Ukraine and other parts of what would one day become the Soviet Union and improved Poland economically and culturally.

One of the First Democracies

Poland was democratic long before most other European countries. Poland's first national parliament met in 1493, and by 1505, Poland had a constitution, unlike France, Russia, or the German kingdoms. The constitution said that the country was legally ruled by a council of noble representatives, chosen by the king and other nobility, who governed in the parliament, or Sejm (SAYM).

By 1569, Poland and Lithuania had joined together in a single parliament. Together, the two countries were strong enough to stand up to their neighbors on all sides.

The nobles of the Sejm were careful to elect kings who would not take away their power. To them the power of the noble class was more important than the strength of the Noble Republic, which was the joint parliament of Poland and Lithuania. After the death in 1572 of the childless Sigismund Augustus II, they wanted a foreign king who would let the nobles keep their power over their own peasants, and at the same time, make certain that no single noble became the ruler of all of the Polish nobility. So in 1587, they finally elected King Sigismund III Vasa, who was also King of Sweden.

Wars Wrack the Country

By the mid-17th century, Poland had become weak because of its ineffective central government and its many wars. The worst wars were with the Islamic Turks, who tried to claim Poland for their Ottoman Empire. The Poles fought the Turks in many battles before King John Sobieski led the forces that defeated them at the Battle of Vienna in 1683. Without this Polish victory, many people think the Islamic religion would have replaced Christianity as the dominant religion in Europe.

After King John Sobieski died in 1696, the Sejm began to elect kings from German Saxony. But descendents of Polish kings also claimed the throne, and neighboring countries thought they too could dictate who ran Poland. This led to the War of Polish Succession from 1733 to 1735. A Saxon king, Augustus III, won the throne, backed by Russia and Germany against Polish nobles and France. His death in 1763 marked the end of Saxon kings in Poland. Because of the Sejm's policy of maintaining the strength of the nobles even at the cost of the strength of the country, in the 226 years of the Noble Republic, seven out of the eleven kings who ruled Poland were foreigners.

The First Partition of Poland — 1772

Stanislaw August Poniatowski, the last king of Poland, was elected in September of 1764. He tried to reform Poland economically and politically and especially made an effort to reform the Sejm.

A special feature of the Sejm was that each member had veto power, so every noble in the Sejm had to agree before something was decided. They usually agreed that the nobility would not have to pay taxes, which made it difficult for the king to pay his army. King Poniatowski tried to convince them to give up their veto, but the nobles even vetoed his attempts to stop the veto! The king was therefore almost bankrupt and could not afford a large army to defend the country.

In 1772, Russia began advancing on this weakened Polish land. Austria and Prussia didn't want Russia to take all of Poland, so Frederick II of Prussia made a treaty with Russia and Austria. As a result, he got Pomerania and part of Great Poland for Prussia, while Russia took Belorussia (Belarus), and Austria got a large part of southern Poland. In this First Partition of Poland, the Poles lost one-third of their lands and half of their population.

Two More Partitions

In 1791, the Sejm created a strong new constitution that would have given Poland a hereditary monarchy. The new constitution took away the veto power that had driven the country to bankruptcy and political weakness. But it was too late.

Catherine II, Empress of Russia, and Frederick II, king of Prussia, joined forces to destroy Poland completely. With her armies ready to attack Polish borders, Catherine II sent her representative to the new Polish Parliament and declared the Second Partition in 1793.

In 1795, the Third Partition of Poland divided Poland among Austria, Russia, and Prussia. Poland was no longer on the map. Russia began to suppress Polish language and culture, as would the Soviet Union after World War II. Partitioned Poland lasted from 1795 to 1918, when US President Woodrow Wilson made Poland's independence one of the conditions for the Armistice, the agreement to end World War I.

Independent Again — But Only Briefly

Poland was independent for 21 years, from 1918 until September 1, 1939, when Nazi Germany's army began World War II by invading Poland. By this time, Russia was part of the Soviet Union, and in 1939, the Soviets were on Germany's side. Like Germany, they wanted Poland back. Adolf Hitler, the leader of Germany, made secret agreements with the Soviet leader, Joseph Stalin, to divide Poland again. But in 1941, the Soviets changed sides and joined the Allies against Germany. When Germany lost the war in 1945, the Soviets kept Poland under their control after liberating it from the Nazis.

Poland was heavily damaged in World War II. Four-fifths of the capital of Warsaw was destroyed. Over six million Poles, including about three million Jews, died during the war or were exterminated in concentration camps. One of the best-known concentration camps, Auschwitz, is near Cracow, along with the larger camp Birkenau. Jews, Gypsies, Poles, and Russian prisoners of war were transported to Auschwitz in sealed cattle cars from all over Europe. Their photographs line the walls of Auschwitz's museum dedicated to remembering the victims of the crimes that were committed there. Over four million people, many of them children, died in the Auschwitz-Birkenau concentration camps.

From 1945 until 1989, the Soviet Union controlled Poland with a communist form of government. Until 1990, it tried to outlaw religion and private enterprise and to suppress the Polish language and culture, requiring schoolchildren to learn Russian. In 1956, the Polish people tried to revolt against the Polish Communist Party, religious repression, and the Soviet Union, but the government was too strong for them.

Solidarity and Freedom in 1989

In 1980, the labor movement Solidarity and its leader, Lech Walesa, began to protest communist control. In response, the government banned the Solidarity organization entirely. But Solidarity continued. Joining with people from the Catholic Church, its members protested against the communist government ruled by General Wojciech Jaruzelski in large street demonstrations and labor strikes. The Catholic Church and Pope John Paul II, himself a Pole, served as mediators and, in 1989, Poland's communist government allowed the people to elect representatives from other political parties. Few members of the Communist Party were reelected, and their government ended. Once again, Poland is a democratic and independent nation.

According to this graffiti, Jaruzelski claims "I only executed orders" in surpressing the Polish independence movement.

In 1990, Poland elected Walesa as president in its first free elections in over 50 years. Walesa was sworn in as Poland's first popularly elected president, and parliament approved his choice of Jan Bielecki as prime minister.

Poland is beginning to change to a capitalist economy after years of state-run stores and factories. Like other countries that change from a communist system, it faces many economic and political problems. While most foods and consumer goods are available, the price of many goods is very high. But the Polish people feel they have won their freedom through their own efforts. As the first country to peacefully break from the former Union of Soviet Socialist Republics and communist domination, Poland hopes to lead the way to a new economic and political order in Eastern Europe.

Government

Poland's National Assembly, or parliament, consists of the 460-member lower house (Sejm) and the upper house (Senate), which has 100 members. The National Assembly's duties are to pass laws and supervise all other branches of government.

The citizen-elected president is the head of state. He supervises foreign policy and chooses a prime minister who must be approved by the Assembly. The president may veto legislation, but his veto can be overturned by a majority vote in the Sejm. The Sejm appoints a Council of Ministers, which heads government departments. Income taxes, special yearly taxes on cars, and taxes on luxury purchases provide revenue for the government. Local government is run by city and town councils.

In December of 1990, Poland had its first free national elections. All adults over the age of 18 were allowed to vote. Previously, under communist rule, everyone was forced to vote, and choices were limited to candidates who were members of the Communist Party. Now the people may choose from any political party.

The government is now in the process of trying to decide how to give every citizen a share in any of several thousand companies previously owned by the state. A number of bills have been proposed in the parliament, but it has been difficult to determine one way of giving shares fairly.

Education

Education is free and compulsory for children from 7 to 15 years of age. Until the 1900s, only a small privileged class could attend school, but now about 98% of all Poles age 15 and over can read and write. For the first seven years of school, Poles attend primary schools. Then, almost all children begin their secondary education at a four-year college preparatory school, a three-year basic vocational training school, or a five-year vocational and technical school.

Graduates of academic or technical schools must pass examinations for entry into universities, technical institutes, or other specialized colleges. Poland has 10 academic universities and more than 50 other institutions of higher education. All are run by the state except for the Roman Catholic University at Lublin, although private universities and schools may now emerge as Poland shifts to a capitalist system.

Population and Ethnic Groups

Poland's population totals approximately 37.5 million people. About half the people live in cities or towns, and the average density of population is about 290 people per square mile (about 750 people per sq km).

Before World War II, Poland was unusual because of the diversity of its ethnic minorities. Ukranians, Belorussians, Germans, Slovaks, Russians, Gypsies, Lithuanians, and about three million Jews made up one-third of the Polish population. Then war deaths, border changes, and massive immigration radically altered the country. Now 98% of the population is Polish of Slavic descent, and only about 6,000 Jews and varying small numbers of other minorities remain. In addition, roughly one Pole of every three now lives outside of Poland.

Land and Climate

Poland covers 120,700 square miles (312,612 sq km), slightly less than half the size of the Canadian province of Manitoba, or about the size of the US state of New Mexico. Its greatest distance from east to west is 430 miles (692 km), and from north to south, 395 miles (636 km). Poland is surrounded by Germany to the west, republics of the former Soviet Union to the east, Czechoslovakia to the south, and the Baltic sea to the north.

Poland has seven major land regions. The coastal lowlands stretch 277 miles (446 km) along the Baltic Sea. The Baltic lakes region is scenic but sparsely populated. More densely populated areas include the agricultural central plains, with the cities of Warsaw, Poznan, and Wrocław; the Polish uplands, which are mineral rich and intensely farmed; and the Carpathian forelands, which include rich farmland, iron and steel industries, and Cracow, the former capital and the region's most important manufacturing and cultural center.

The low, forested Sudetes (Sudeten) Mountains contain farming valleys and textile towns. Rysy Peak, at 8,199 feet (2,499 m) in the western Carpathian Mountains, is Poland's highest point. The Carpathian mountains and Baltic Sea offer Poland its only natural protection from invasion.

Poland's coast has milder weather than inland, but winters throughout Poland are cold with heavy snow. Summers are warm with moderate rainfall averaging 24 inches (61 cm) a year. The average high temperature in Warsaw is 31°F (-1°C) in January, compared to 75°F (24°C) in July.

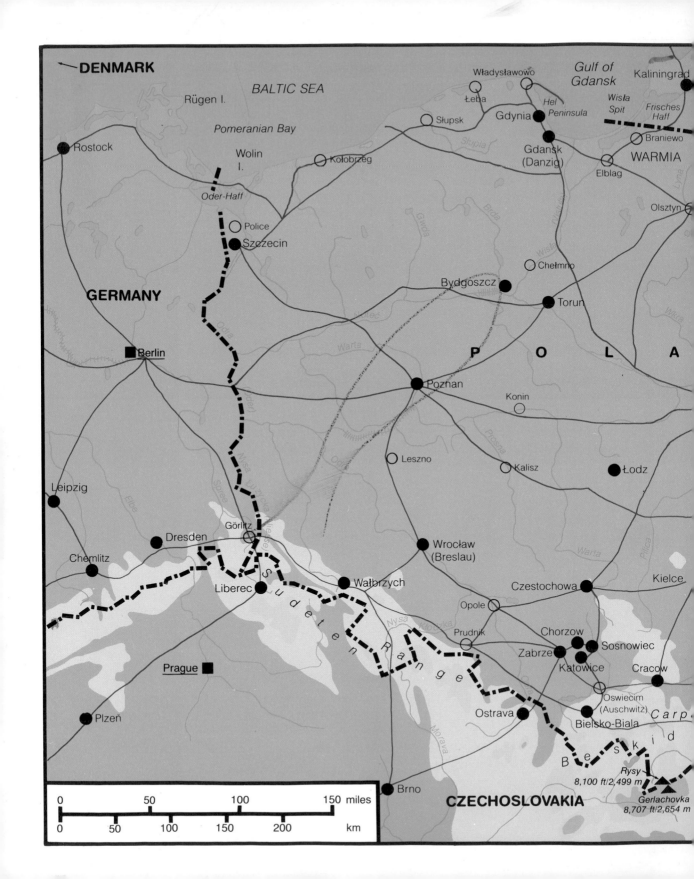

POLAND – Political and Physical

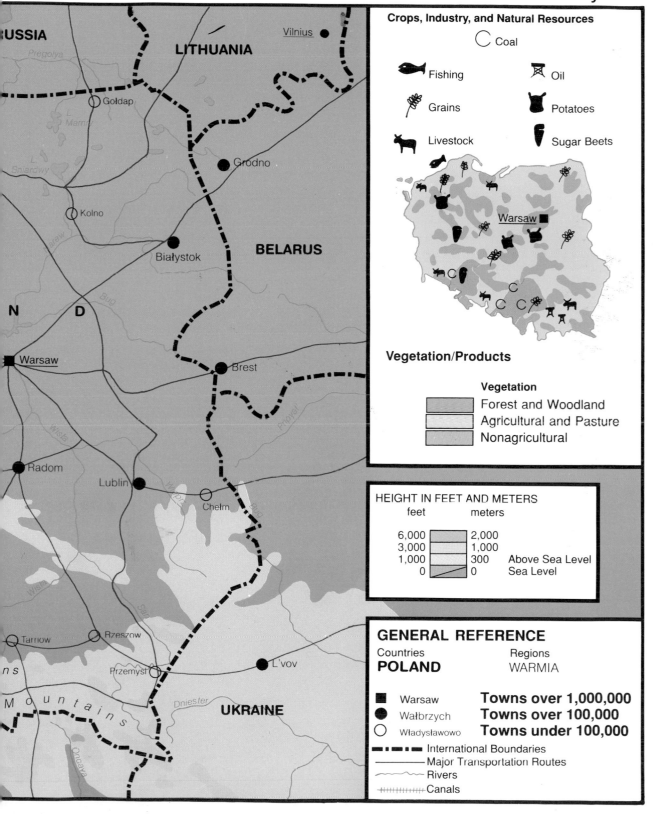

RUSSIA

LITHUANIA

Vilnius

Pregolya

Gołdap

L. Mamry

L. Śniardwy

Grodno

Kolno

BELARUS

Białystok

Bug

N **D**

Warsaw

Brest

Wisła

Pripyat'

Radom

Lublin

Wieprz

Chełm

Wisła

Bug

San

Tarnow

Rzeszow

Przemyśl

L'vov

Mountains

Dniester

UKRAINE

Oncava

Crops, Industry, and Natural Resources

- ◠ Coal
- 🐟 Fishing
- ⌗ Oil
- 🌾 Grains
- Potatoes
- 🐎 Livestock
- Sugar Beets

Warsaw

Vegetation/Products

Vegetation
- Forest and Woodland
- Agricultural and Pasture
- Nonagricultural

HEIGHT IN FEET AND METERS

feet	meters	
6,000	2,000	
3,000	1,000	
1,000	300	Above Sea Level
0	0	Sea Level

GENERAL REFERENCE

Countries	Regions
POLAND	WARMIA

- ■ Warsaw **Towns over 1,000,000**
- ● Wałbrzych **Towns over 100,000**
- ○ Władysławowo **Towns under 100,000**
- ▪–▪– International Boundaries
- ——— Major Transportation Routes
- ～～～ Rivers
- ++++++ Canals

Natural Resources, Agriculture, and Industry

Poland is a leading producer of coal, its chief natural resource and primary source of electrical power. It also mines sulfur, copper, salt, lead, and zinc and has small amounts of natural gas and petroleum.

Three-fifths of Poland is farmland. In spite of its poor soil, Poland is second only to the republics of the former Soviet Union in production of potatoes and rye. It also grows barley, sugar beets, and wheat. Most farmers raise hogs, but a few cattle and sheep farmers are primarily found in the hilly regions of the south. Large hand-carved rakes and horse-drawn wagons are still commonly used to harvest crops, although some more modern farm machinery is used as well. Most farms are small, family-owned plots that were never made into communist-style collective farms.

The communist government owned over 90% of Polish industries until 1989, but now the new government is trying to give individuals more ownership of the factories. Food and consumer goods are in chronically short supply, but the new government is trying to change this. Chemicals, food products, machinery, ships, textiles, iron, and steel are Poland's chief manufactured products. One of the largest steel foundries in the world is at Nowa Huta, near Cracow, where over half of Poland's steel and iron is produced. The major portion of Poland's commercial fishing catch is herring and cod. The lumber industry relies on the north country and Carpathian slopes for its timber, wood pulp, and paper production.

Poland's chief exports are coal, food products, machinery, ships, and sulfur. It imports cotton, food products, iron ore, machinery, petroleum, wool, and other goods.

Currency

The basic unit of money in Poland is the *złoty*, which is equal to 100 *groszy*. Because of tremendous inflation since the country's independence, in 1992, 10,000 złoty were equal to one US dollar or 1.11 Canadian dollars. So 1,000 złoty notes are considered small change. A 50,000 złoty note equals about five US dollars.

Language

Poland's major language is Polish, a Western Slavic language. Unlike other Slavic languages such as Russian and Bulgarian, which use the Cyrillic alphabet, Polish is written in the same Roman alphabet as English. Some accents, unusual letter combinations such as *sz*, *cz*, *rz*, *dz*, and a special letter *ł* make Polish spelling unusual. In addition, *w* makes a *v* sound, *j* makes the *y* sound of *yes*, and *c* stands for *ts*.

Religion

About 94% of Poles practice Roman Catholicism, while the remainder are Russian Orthodox, Protestant, or Jewish. Under communism, religious freedom was supposed to be guaranteed, but the communist regime tried unsuccessfully to limit the Catholic Church. In 1978, Pope John Paul II was elected the first pope from Poland. He still draws immense crowds when he visits his homeland, especially when he visits Jasna Gora.

The Black Madonna of Jasna Gora at Czestochowa is a painting dressed in jewels that has been the focus of religious pilgrimages for over six centuries. Two slashes mar the right cheek of the Madonna, caused by religious dissenters' swords that slashed into the painting in 1430, according to legend. In May and throughout the summer, large groups of young people walk from all over Poland in a special pilgrimage to worship at the shrine of the Black Madonna.

Art and Culture

Religion and literature have long been the twin pillars of Polish culture. Nicholas Rey is considered the father of Polish literature because he and Jan Kochanowski were among the first to use Polish language for their works, bringing Poland a golden age of literature in the 16th century. The 19th-century poet Adam Mickiewicz is best known for his patriotic verse in Polish, while Teodor Jozef Konrad Korzeniowski wrote his novels in English under the well-known name of Joseph Conrad. Praised for his short stories, which include many tales from his childhood in the prewar Jewish towns of Poland, Isaac Bashevis Singer won the Nobel Prize for literature in 1979.

Poland's major contributions to science include Nicholas Copernicus' sun-centered model of the solar system and Marie Curie-Skłodowska's co-discovery of radium and the naturally radioactive metallic element polonium. She and her husband, Pierre Curie, named the element after her native country.

Today, Polish artists are internationally known for their vibrant visual arts and posters. The arts, including theater, dance, and music, were generously funded under communist rule and have flourished in Poland as a result.

Sports and Recreation

As in most European countries, soccer is a national passion in Poland. Poles also play basketball, volleyball, and tennis. Sailing, mountain climbing, skiing, gymnastics, and horseback riding are favorite forms of recreation. While ballroom and folk dance are popular, Polish youth eagerly seek western rock and roll. They buy tapes from street vendors and hear the latest music on their radios. Those with satellite television are able to see rock videos and follow the career of their own international rock star, Basia.

Warsaw

Warsaw's motto, "It defies the storms," defines this capital's history. The city recovered from occupation by Swedish and Prussian armies during 1655-56 only to be assaulted by the Russians in 1794. In 1939, Nazis bombed the city until it surrendered, carried off its art treasures, and sent many of its citizens to German labor or concentration camps. When the citizens rebelled — the Jews in 1943 and many other citizens in the Polish resistance of 1944 — the Nazis systematically killed or deported the people and destroyed the city.

Now Warsaw flourishes once again as a center for social, cultural, educational, and political activities and as the hub of the transportation network linking Poland to the rest of Europe. In the Old City, Market Square houses were reconstructed according to their 15th-century original design, and churches and castles of later periods have been rebuilt. Outside the Old City sprawl apartment buildings and industrial centers of modern design.

Poles in North America

Polish migration to the United States and Canada was not significant until after 1850, when Poles began to leave Prussian-controlled sectors of Poland (where German was spoken) because of the Partitions. Because they understood German, they tended to move to cities where many Germans lived such as Chicago, Milwaukee, Cleveland, and Buffalo. After 1890, frustrated by the foreign stranglehold on their country, Poles migrated from the Austrian and Russian-controlled sectors of partitioned Poland. Today, Chicago boasts more Poles than now live in the city of Warsaw, while urban regions of Ontario in Canada have provided work for many Polish immigrants.

Glossary of Important Terms

collective farm .... m or group of farms worked
cooperatively by laborers supervised
by the government.

commemorate ....to honor the memory of something
or someone.

foreland...a projecting land mass.

kiosk ....a small stand or booth.

partition ....the act of dividing into sections.

row houses...a series of identical houses built
side by side and joined by a
common wall.

therapy...treatment of mental, emotional,
and nervous illnesses, often by
talking about past and ongoing
problems with a trained counselor.

Glossary of Useful Polish Terms

chłopiec (HWAHP-yets) ....boy
do widzenie (Doh veed-ZEN-ya) ....good-bye
dziekuje bardzo (jen-KOO-ya BARD-zo) ..thank you very much
dzie′n dobry (jen DOB-ree) ....good morning, good day
dziewczynka (jev-CHIN-ka) ....girl
matka (MAHT-ka) ....mother
nauczyciel (nah-OH-chee-chel) ....teacher
nie (NEE-eh)...no
ojciec (OYTS-yets) ....father
prosze bardzo (PRASH-uh BARD-zo).........you are welcome
szkoła (SHKO-wa) ....school
tak (TAHK) ....yes

More Books about Poland

The Land and People of Poland. Kelly (J.B. Lippincott)
Lech Walesa — The Leader of Solidarity and Campaigner for Freedom and
    Human Rights in Poland. Craig (Gareth Stevens)
Poland. Brandys (Doubleday)
Poland. Greene (Childrens Press)
Polish Greats. Madison (David McKay)
World at War — Invasion of Poland. Skipper (Children s Press)

Things To Do — Research Projects and Activities

Many different rulers and countries have dominated Poland over its long history. Now Poland has changed again, from a communist government and economy to capitalist ones. How will the Polish people adapt to these changes? To find this out — and to work on the projects listed below — you will need up-to-date information. Use the following guides to find recent articles on Poland and other subjects:

Readers' Guide to Periodical Literature
Children's Magazine Guide

1. Polish armies had to fight invaders throughout Poland's history. In the 1600s, Hussar soldiers wore armor with feathers attached that made a buzzing noise when they rode into battle. This helped frighten their enemies. Compare this battle dress with that worn in other countries in the past. What do modern soldiers wear, and how does it protect them?

2. Find out more about one of Poland's world-famous scientists, such as Nicolai Copernicus or Marie Curie-Skłodowska. When did the scientist live and study, and what did he or she do to contribute to science?

3. Get recordings of Polish composer Frédéric Chopin's compositions from the library and see why people have considered his music so special for over 100 years.

4. Isaac Bashevis Singer wrote about his native Poland for children as well as adults. Get a copy of his *Stories for Children Collection*. Can you retell a story of his in your own words? How would you illustrate it?

5. Poland is geographically and culturally a bridge between east and west in Europe. What countries are truly considered members of eastern Europe? Western Europe? In what ways are western European countries different from eastern ones? How does Poland combine the two?

6. If you would like a pen pal in Poland, write to either of these two groups:

International Pen Friends   Worldwide Pen Friends
P.O. Box 290065   P.O. Box 39097
Brooklyn, NY 11229   Downey, CA 90241

Be sure to tell them what country you want your pen pal to be from. Also include your full name, age, and address.

Index

agriculture 58
Allies 52
architecture 60
arts 34, 59, 60
Auschwitz 24, 25, 52
Austria 26, 51, 52, 60

Baltic Sea 55
Basia 60
Belorussia (Belarus) 51
Belorussians 55
Birkenau 52
Bolesław the Brave 49
Buffalo 60

Canada 60
Carpathian Mountains 55
Casimir the Great 49-50
Catherine II 52
Chicago 60
chores 42-43
Cleveland 60
climate 55
communism 12, 26-27, 33, 34, 39, 53, 54, 58, 60
concentration camps 24, 52, 60
Conrad, Joseph 59
constitution 52
Copernicus, Nicholas 59
Cracow 36, 48, 50, 55, 58
culture 59
Curie, Pierre 59
Curie-Skłodowska, Marie 59
currency 58
Czechoslovakia 49, 55
Czestochowa 59

economy 26, 31, 33, 53, 54
education 22, 46, 53, 54
elections 27, 53, 54
ethnic groups 55

Europe 48, 49, 53

farming 29
First Partition of Poland 51-52
flowers 18-19, 30
food 40
France 50, 51
Frederick II 52

Gdansk 39
Germany 24, 26, 49, 50, 51, 52, 55
government 26, 33, 50, 51, 53, 54, 58
Grunwald, Battle of 50
Gypsies 52, 55

history 48-53
Hitler, Adolf 24, 52
holidays 24
Holocaust 25
housing 10, 12-13, 16, 18, 31, 60

industry 58

Jadwiga 50
Jagiello 50
Jaruzelski, General Wojciech 53
Jews 24, 25, 52, 55, 59, 60

King Augustus III 51
King John Sobieski 51
King Louis of Hungary 50
King Sigismund Augustus II 50
King Sigismund III Vasa 51
King Stanislaw August Poniatowski 51
Kochanowski, Jan 59

labor unions 27
Ladislas the Short 49

land 55
LANGUAGES 59: English 7, 16, 59;
    German 60; Polish 7, 22, 34, 59;
    Russian 7, 22, 53, 59
legends 33, 36
Lenin, Vladimir 26
Lithuania 50, 55

Manitoba 55
Mickiewicz, Adam 59
Mieszko I 49
migration 60
Milwaukee 7, 60
Mongolia 49

natural resources 58
Nazis 24-26, 52, 60
New Mexico 55
nobility 50-51
Noble Republic 50, 51
Nowa Huta 58

Ontario 60

Palaces of Culture 34
parliament 50, 51, 52, 54
pets 10
physics 6, 15
Piasts 49-50
Polish names 6
Polish Succession, War of 51
politics 26-27, 53
Pope John Paul II 39, 53, 59
population 55
Poznan 6, 15, 26, 30, 31, 33, 36,
    45, 55
Protestantism 59
Prussia 26, 51, 52, 60
psychology 14

recreation 44-45, 46, 60

religion 39, 53, 59
religious shrines 19, 39, 59
Rey, Nicholas 59
rock and roll 60
Roman Catholicism 39, 49, 50,
    53, 59
Russia 26, 49, 50, 51, 52, 60
Russian Orthodoxy 59
Russians 52, 55
Rysy Peak 55

Second Partition of Poland 52
Singer, Isaac Bashevis 59
Slavonic tribes 49
Slovaks 55
Solidarity 27, 53
Soviet Union 12, 26-27, 34, 49,
    52, 53, 55, 58
sports 10, 60
Stalin, Joseph 52
Sudetes (Sudeten) Mountains 55
Sweden 51, 60

Tartars 36, 49
television 45, 46
Teutonic knights 50
Third Partition of Poland 52
Turks 51

Ukranians 55
United States 7, 15, 60
universities 54

Walesa, Lech 53
war memorials 19, 24, 25, 26, 52
Warsaw 24, 52, 55, 60
Wilson, Woodrow 52
World War I 26, 52
World War II 12, 24, 26, 31, 33,
    52, 55
Wrocław 55